STAR WARS®
WORKBOOKS

ALPHABET AND PHONICS

FOR AGES 5-6

BY THE EDITORS OF BRAIN QUEST

CONSULTING EDITOR: DALE BLAESS

SCHOLASTIC

Scholastic Children's Books
Euston House,
24 Eversholt Street,
London NW1 1DB, UK

A division of Scholastic Ltd
London ~ New York ~ Toronto ~ Sydney ~ Auckland
Mexico City ~ New Delhi ~ Hong Kong

First published in the USA by Workman Publishing in 2014.
This edition published in the UK by Scholastic Ltd in 2015.

© & TM 2015 LUCASFILM LTD.

STAR WARS is a registered trademark of Lucasfilm Ltd.
BRAIN QUEST is a registered trademark of Workman Publishing Co., Inc., and Groupe Play Bac, S.A.

Workbook series design by Raquel Jaramillo
Cover illustration by Mike Sutfin
Interior illustrations by Mark Poutenis

ISBN 978 1407 16278 2

Printed and bound by Bell & Bain Ltd, United Kingdom

2 4 6 8 10 9 7 5 3

Papers used by Scholastic Children's Books are made from woods grown in sustainable forests.

www.scholastic.co.uk

WORKBOOKS

This workbook belongs to:

BEN

_____

A Anakin

Anakin begins with the **A** sound.

Say the word for each picture.

Circle the pictures that begin with the **A** sound.

Boba Fett

B

Boba begins with the **B** sound.

Say the word for each picture.

Circle the pictures that begin with the **B** sound.

C Clone trooper

Clone begins with the **C** sound.

Say the word for each picture.

Circle the pictures that begin with the **C** sound.

Droid

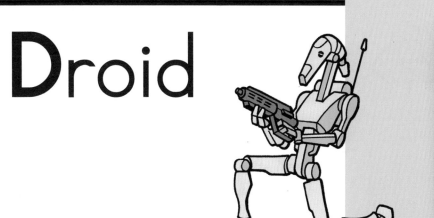

Droid begins with the **D** sound.

Say the word for each picture.

Circle the pictures that begin with the **D** sound.

E Emperor Palpatine

Emperor begins with the **E** sound.

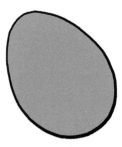

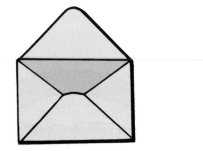

Say the word for each picture.

Circle the pictures that begin with the **E** sound.

Kit Fisto

F

Fisto begins with the **F** sound.

Say the word for each picture.

Circle the pictures that begin with the **F** sound.

G Greedo

Greedo begins with the **G** sound.

Say the word for each picture.

Circle the pictures that begin with the **G** sound.

Han Solo

H

Han begins with the **H** sound.

Say the word for each picture.

Circle the pictures that begin with the **H** sound.

Imperial Guard

Imperial begins with the **I** sound.

Say the word for each picture.

Circle the pictures that begin with the **I** sound.

Jar Jar Binks

J

Jar Jar begins with the J sound.

Say the word for each picture.

Circle the pictures that begin with the J sound.

K Ki-Adi-Mundi

Ki-Adi-Mundi begins with the **K** sound.

Say the word for each picture.

Circle the pictures that begin with the **K** sound.

Luke Skywalker

Luke begins with the L sound.

Say the word for each picture.

Circle the pictures that begin with the L sound.

M Mace Windu

Mace begins with the **M** sound.

  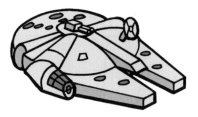

Say the word for each picture.

Circle the pictures that begin with the **M** sound.

Nute Gunray

Nute begins with the **N** sound.

Say the word for each picture.

Circle the pictures that begin with the **N** sound.

O Obi-Wan Kenobi

Obi-Wan begins with the **O** sound.

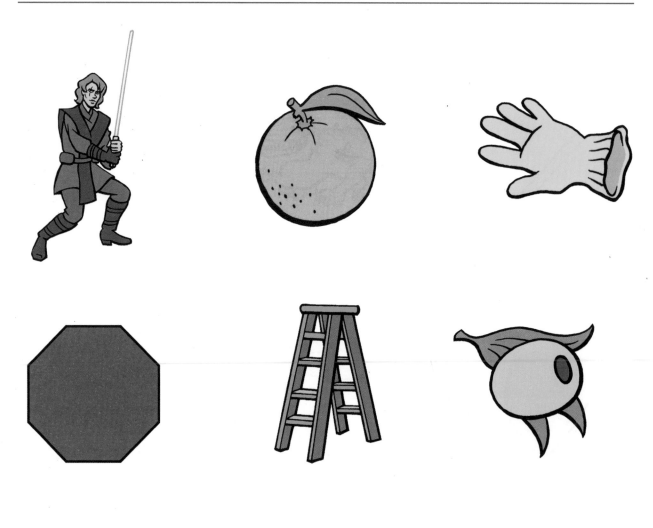

Say the word for each picture.

Circle the pictures that begin with the **O** sound.

Plo Koon

P

Plo begins with the **P** sound.

Say the word for each picture.

Circle the pictures that begin with the **P** sound.

Q Queen Amidala

Queen begins with the **Q** sound.

Say the word for each picture.

Circle the pictures that begin with the **Q** sound.

Reek

R

Reek begins with the **R** sound.

Say the word for each picture.

Circle the pictures that begin with the **R** sound.

S Storm-trooper

Stormtrooper begins with the **S** sound.

Say the word for each picture.

Circle the pictures that begin with the **S** sound.

Tusken Raider

T

Tusken begins with the **T** sound.

 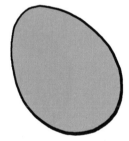 

Say the word for each picture.

Circle the pictures that begin with the **T** sound.

U

Luminara Unduli

Unduli begins with the **U** sound.

  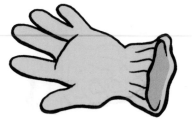

Say the word for each picture.

Circle the pictures that begin with the **U** sound.

Vader

Vader begins with the **V** sound.

Say the word for each picture.

Circle the pictures that begin with the **V** sound.

W Wookiee

Wookiee begins with the **W** sound.

Say the word for each picture.

Circle the pictures that begin with the **W** sound.

X-wing

X-wing begins with the **X** sound.

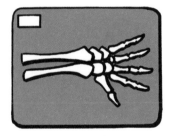

Say the word for each picture.

Circle the pictures that begin with the **X** sound.

Y  Yoda

Yoda begins with the **Y** sound.

Say the word for each picture.

Circle the pictures that begin with the **Y** sound.

Zam Wesell

Zam begins with the **Z** sound.

Say the word for each picture.

Circle the pictures that begin with the **Z** sound.

Short a

The first **a** in **acklay** has the **short a** sound.

Circle the pictures that have the same **short a** sound as **acklay**.

Short e

Jedi has the **short e** sound.

Circle the pictures that have the same **short e** sound as **Jedi**.

Short i

Wicket has the **short i** sound.

Circle the pictures that have the same **short i** sound as **Wicket**.

Short o

Podracer has the short o sound.

Circle the pictures that have the same short o sound as podracer.

Short u

Hutt has the **short u** sound.

Circle the pictures that have the same **short u** sound as **Hutt**.

Long a

Vader has the long a sound.

Circle the pictures that have the same long a sound as Vader.

Long e

Queen has the **long e** sound.

Circle the pictures that have the same **long e** sound as **queen**.

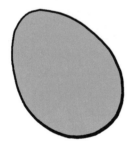

Long i

Qui-Gon has the **long i** sound.

Circle the pictures that have the same **long i** sound as **Qui-Gon**.

Long o

Yoda has the **long o** sound.

Circle the pictures that have
the same **long o** sound as **Yoda**.

Long u

Luke has the **long u** sound.

Circle the pictures that have
the same **long u** sound as **Luke**.

Short and Long

These sentences all have **short** and **long** sounds for the same vowel.

Draw a line underneath the letters with the **long sound**.

Draw a circle around the letters with the **short sound**.

A

Vader found the hat in the cave.

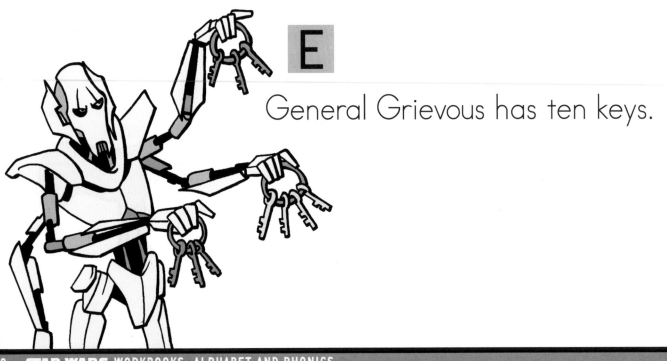

E

General Grievous has ten keys.

I

Qui-Gon Jinn sees a ship on fire.

O

Lobot puts a rope in a box.

U

Luminara Unduli sees a blue sun.

y

The letter **y** can have two sounds:
a **long i** sound, or a **long e** sound.

Draw a box around the pictures that end
with the **long i** sound.

Draw a circle around the pictures that end
with the **long e** sound.

sky

lady

cry

fly

city

baby

ch

When **c** and **h** are next to each other, they come together to make a new sound: **ch**.

Say the word for each picture.

Circle the pictures that begin with the **ch** sound.

Chewbacca

Chewbacca begins with the **ch** sound.

sh

When **s** and **h** are next to each other, they come together to make a new sound: **sh**.

Say the word for each picture.

Circle the pictures that begin with the **sh** sound.

Shmi

Shmi begins with the **sh** sound.

th

When t and h are next to each other, they come together to make a new sound: th.

Say the word for each picture.

Circle the pictures that begin or end with the th sound.

Darth

Darth ends with the **th** sound.

Soft c

The letter **c** has two sounds.

You can hear the **soft c** sound in the word **Mace**.

Say the word for each picture.

Fill in the **c** to complete each **soft c** word.

Mace

If the **c** comes before an **e**, **i** or **y**, it usually takes the sound of the letter **s**.

ity

prin ess

ereal

podra er

Hard c

The letter **c** has two sounds.

You can hear the **hard c** sound in the word **Count**.

Say the word for each picture.

Fill in the **c** to complete each **hard c** word.

Count Dooku

If the **c** comes before a consonant or the vowels **a**, **o** or **u**, it usually takes the sound of the letter **k**.

_loud

_lone trooper

bla_k

_Lando _alrissian

Soft g

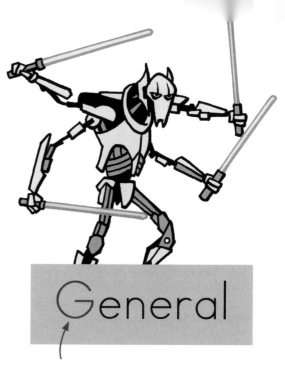

The letter **g** has two sounds.

You can hear the **soft g** sound in the word **General**.

Say the word for each picture.

Copy the **soft g** word on the lines below.

General

If the **g** comes before an **e**, **i** or **y**, it usually takes the sound of the letter **j**.

 bridge

_____

- - - - - - - - - - - - - - - - - - -

_____

 Geonosian

_____

- - - - - - - - - - - - - - - - - - -

_____

 gemstone

_____

- - - - - - - - - - - - - - - - - - -

_____

Hard g

The letter **g** has two sounds.

You can hear the **hard g** sound in the word **Greedo**.

Say the word for each picture.

Copy the **hard g** word on the lines below.

Greedo

If the **g** comes before a consonant, or the vowels **a**, **o** or **u**, it usually takes the sound of a hard **g**.

goat

galaxy

green

Names

Say the name of each character.

What is the first sound you hear?

Write the letter that makes that sound.

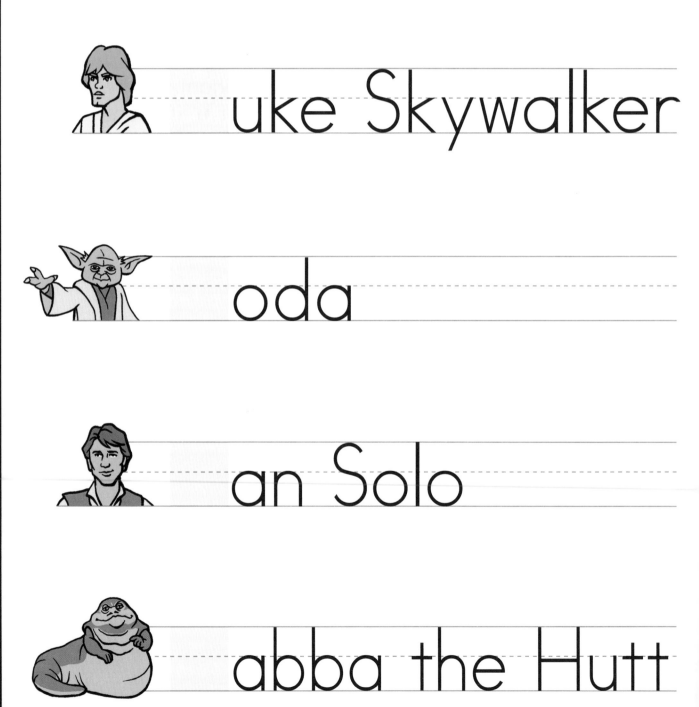

_uke Skywalker

_oda

_an Solo

_abba the Hutt

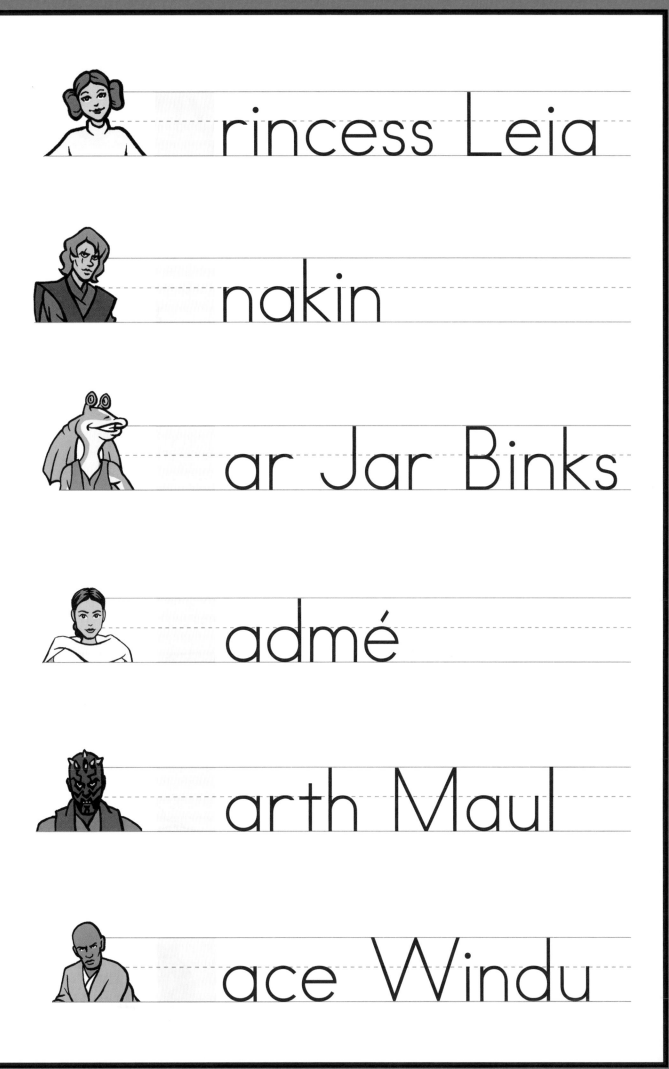

rincess Leia

nakin

ar Jar Binks

admé

arth Maul

ace Windu

Colour Rhyme!

Each of the **colours** rhymes with one of the pictures.

Draw a line from each colour to its rhyming picture.

Rhyme Time!

Each of the pictures in the left column rhymes with one of the pictures in the right column.

Draw a line from each picture on the left to its rhyming picture on the right.

b, d and f

These people, creatures, and things all start with the b, d or f sound.

Say the word for each picture. What beginning sound do you hear?

Write the letter.

ewback

oot

antha

ox

roid

Boba ett

ancer

ire

esert

oy

h, j and k

These people, creatures and things all start with the **h**, **j** or **k** sound.

Say the word for each picture.

What beginning sound do you hear?

Write the letter.

elmet

ar

ing

an

and

ug

ump

ite

ick

unk

m and n

These people, creatures and things all start with the **m** or **n** sound.

Say the word for each picture.

What beginning sound do you hear?

Write the letter.

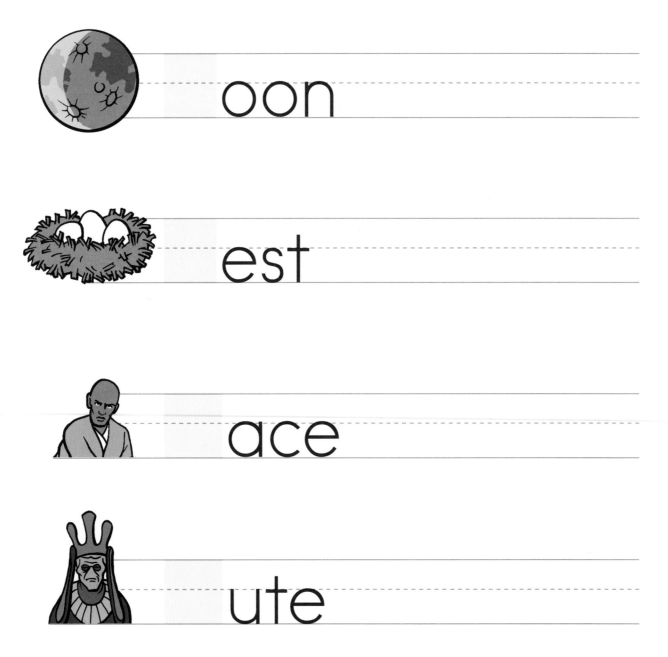

oon

est

ace

ute

an

9 ine

ose

ug

ynock

exu

r, s and t

These creatures and things all start with the
r, **s** or **t** sound.

Say the word for each picture.

What beginning sound do you hear?

Write the letter.

eek

tarship

tormtrooper

usken Raider

poon

auntaun

oes

7 even

riangle

ancor

v, w, x, y and z

These people, creatures and things all start with the **v**, **w**, **x**, **y** or **z** sound.

Say the word for each picture.

What beginning sound do you hear?

Write the letter.

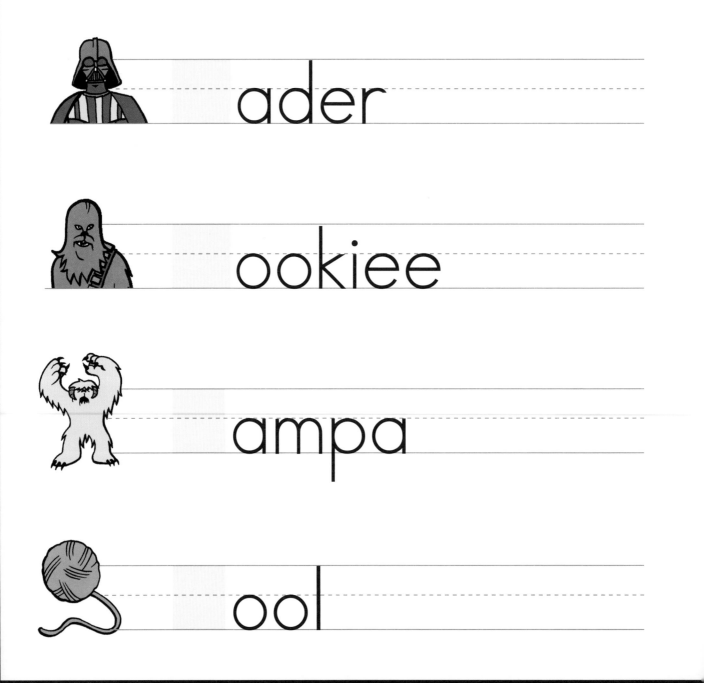

_____ ader

_____ ookiee

_____ ampa

_____ ool

―wing

oda

am Wesell

ip

olcano

―ray

b or d?

The words for these pictures all end in **b** or **d**.

Say the word for each picture.

What ending sound do you hear?

Write the letter.

droi

bathtu

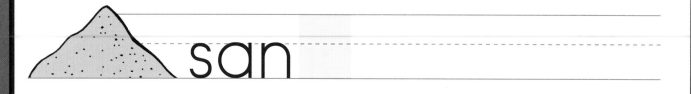

san

Bi Fortuna

m or n?

The words for these pictures all end in **m** or **n**.

Say the word for each picture.

What ending sound do you hear?

Write the letter.

 moo

 Anaki

 dru

 Za   Wesell

p or t?

The words for these pictures all end in p or t.

Say the word for each picture.

What ending sound do you hear?

Write the letter.

starshi

Lobo

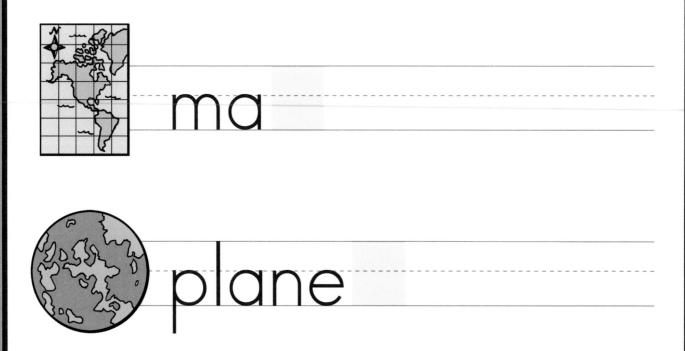

ma

plane

r or s?

The words for these pictures all end in **r** or **s**.

Say the word for each picture.

What ending sound do you hear?

Write the letter.

ca

sta

Jar Jar Bink

bu

g or k?

The words for these pictures all end in **g** or **k**.

Say the word for each picture.

What ending sound do you hear?

Write the letter.

ree

fla

do

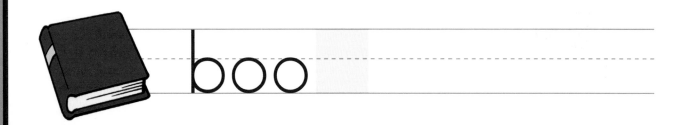

boo

Sight Words

Some words are used a lot. Read each of these sight words out loud.

I

you

me

my

we

am

a

the

is

are

he

she

it

and

for

has

on

under

can

do

in

out

here

there

look

one

go

to

up

down

please

play

said

I

Say the sight word **I**.
Trace and then write the word **I**.

I

Write **I** to complete the sentences.

_____ am a child.

_____ like *Star Wars*.

_____ like to play.

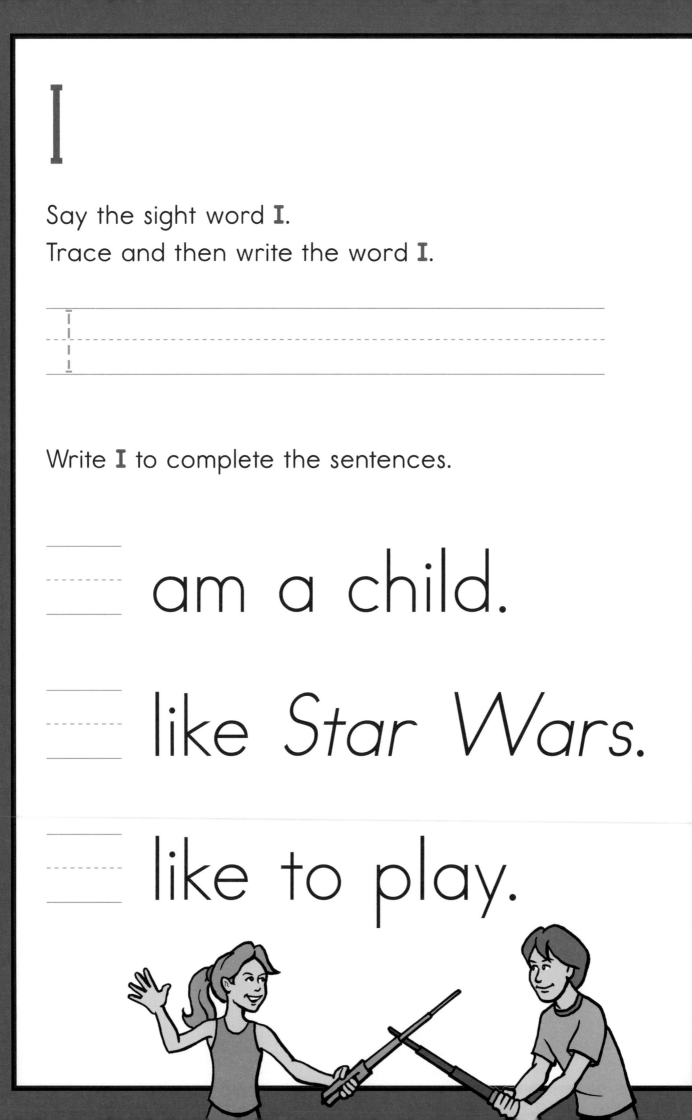

you

Say the sight word **you**.
Trace and then write the word **you**.

you

Write **you** to complete the sentences.

Are _____ excited?

Are _____ sad?

Are _____ cold?

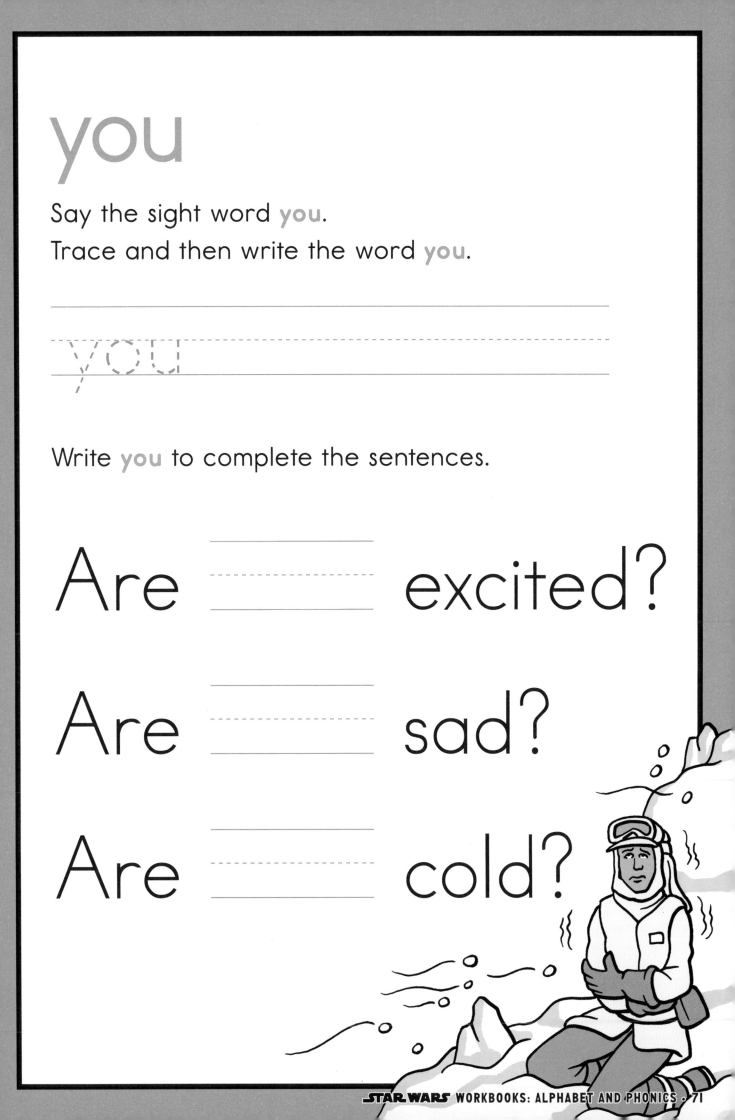

me

Say the sight word **me**.
Trace and then write the word **me**.

me

Write **me** to complete the sentences.

My family loves ____.

Jar Jar makes ____

laugh.

my

Say the sight word my.
Trace and then write the word my.

my

Draw your favourite
Star Wars character
in the box.

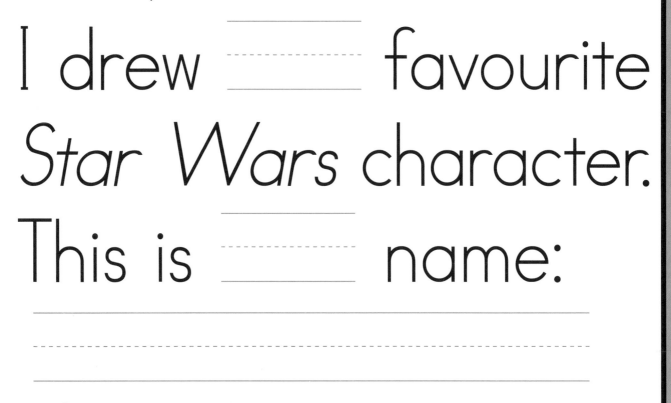

Write my to complete the sentences.
Then write your name.

I drew _____ favourite
Star Wars character.
This is _____ name:

we

Say the sight word **we**.
Trace and then write the word **we**.

we

Write **we** to complete the sentences.

Where are ____?

Here ____ go!

Can ____ watch
Star Wars?

am

Say the sight word **am**.
Trace and then write the word **am**.

am

Write **am** to describe what you are doing.

I _____ reading.

I _____ playing.

a

Say the sight word **a**.

Trace and then write the word **a**.

These children are dressed as *Star Wars* characters!
Write **a** to describe them.

I am _____ Wookiee.

I am _____ Jawa.

I am _____ Jedi.

I am _____ droid.

the

Say the sight word **the**.
Trace and then write the word **the**.

Write **the** to complete the sentences.

This is _____ Death Star.

He is Jabba _____ Hutt.

is

Say the sight word **is**.
Trace and then write the word **is**.

is

Write **is** to describe the weather.

It _____ sunny today.

It _____ not raining.

are

Say the sight word are.
Trace and then write the word are.

are

Write are to complete the sentences.

The Ewoks _____ building.

The Ewoks _____ dancing.

he

Say the sight word **he**.
Trace and then write the word **he**.

he

Write **he** to talk about Luke.

Does _____ like to use the Force?

Yes, _____ likes to use the Force.

she

Say the sight word **she**.
Trace and then write the word **she**.

she

Write **she** to talk about Leia.

Does _____ like to rescue people?

Yes, _____ likes to rescue people.

it

Say the sight word it.
Trace and then write the word it.

it

The word it tells us about an object.
Write it to tell us about this object.

Does _____ fly?

Yes, _____ flies.

and

Say the sight word **and**.
Trace and then write the word **and**.

and

The word **and** connects words.
Write **and** to connect these friends.

Han Solo _____
Chewbacca are
friends.

Leia _____ Luke
are friends.

for

Say the sight word **for**.
Trace and then write the word **for**.

for

Who are these presents **for**?
Write **for** to complete the sentences.

This present
is _____ Anakin!

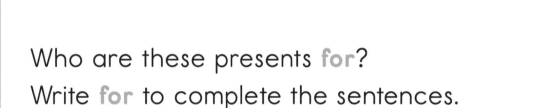

This present
is _____ Padmé!

has

Say the sight word has.
Trace and then write the word has.

has

Jango Fett has a lot of things.
Write has to complete the sentences.

He _____ a son.

He _____ a starship.

on

Say the sight word **on**.
Trace and then write the word **on**.

on

Write **on** to complete the sentences.

Jar Jar is standing _____ a rock.

The ball is _____ his head.

under

Say the sight word **under**.
Trace and then write the word **under**.

under

Write **under** to complete the sentences.

Jar Jar is hiding

_____

_____ a bantha.

They are

_____

_____

a tree.

can

Say the sight word **can**.
Trace and then write the word **can**.

can

Write **can** to complete the sentences.

The youngling _____ climb trees.

The Ewok _____ help him.

do

Say the sight word **do**.
Trace and then write the word **do**.

do

Write **do** to complete the sentences.

What is your favourite thing to _____ ?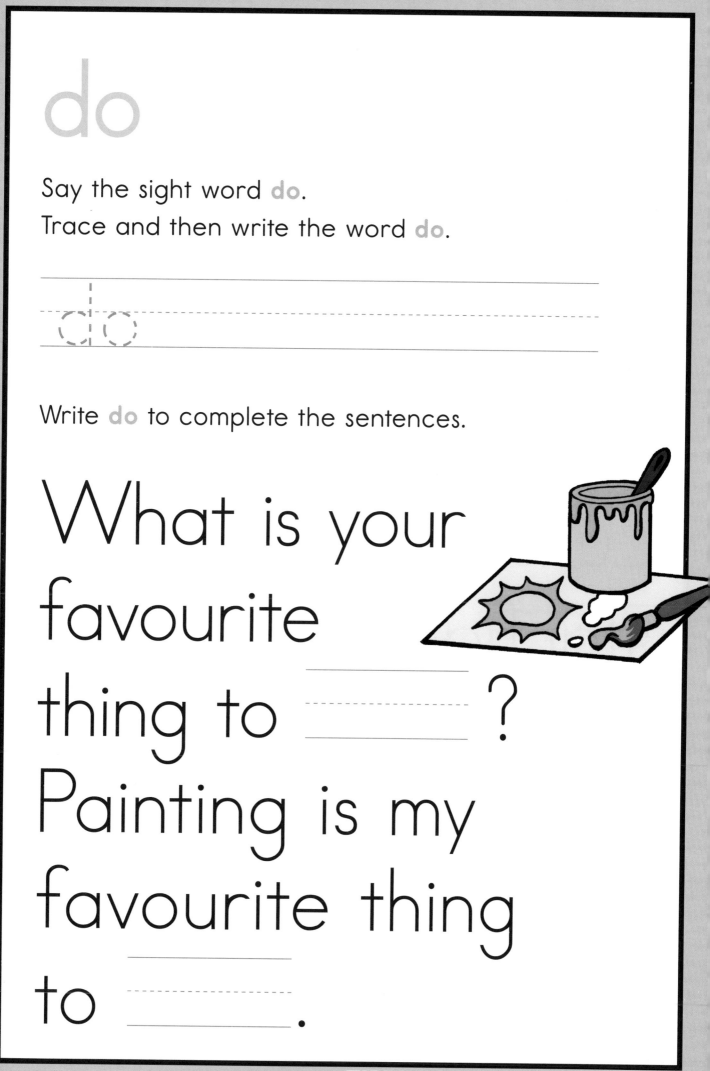
Painting is my favourite thing to _____ .

in

Say the sight word **in**.

Trace and then write the word **in**.

in

Write **in** to tell us where Luke is.

Luke is ____ the starfighter.

Luke is ____ danger.

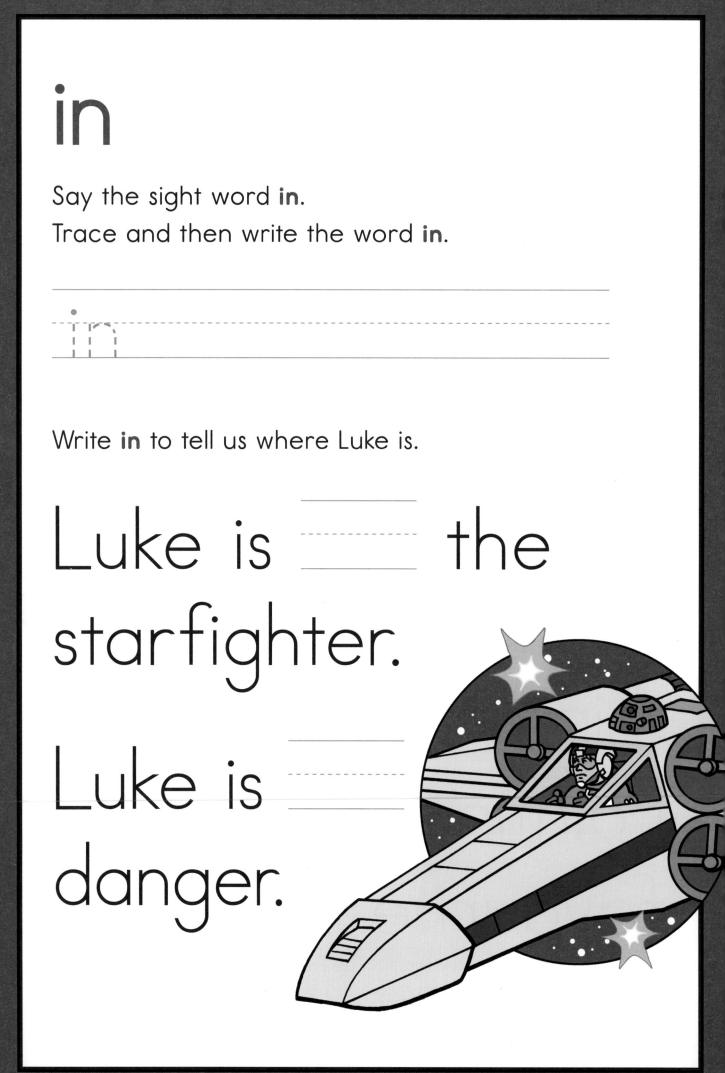

out

Say the sight word **out**.
Trace and then write the word **out**.

out

Write **out** to tell us where Luke is.

Luke gets _____ of the starfighter.

Luke is _____ of danger.

here

Say the sight word **here**.
Trace and then write the word **here**.

here

Where is Chewbacca?
Write **here** to tell us where Chewbacca is.

Chewbacca is _____.

there

Say the sight word there.
Trace and then write the word there.

there

Where is Chewbacca?
Write there to tell us where Chewbacca is.

Chewbacca

is _____.

look

Say the sight word **look**.
Trace and then write the word **look**.

look

C-3PO and R2-D2 **look** through a telescope.
Write **look** to complete the sentences.

They _____
at Kamino.
They _____
at Endor.

one

Say the sight word **one**.
Trace and then write the word **one**.

one

How many things does Obi-Wan have?
Write **one** to complete the sentence.

Obi-Wan has
lightsaber and sees
droid.

go

Say the sight word **go**.

Trace and then write the word **go**.

Where are R2-D2 and C-3PO going?

Write **go** to complete the sentence.

They ___ to the desert.

to

Say the sight word **to**.
Trace and then write the word **to**.

t̶o̶

Where is Princess Leia going?
Write **to** to complete the sentence.

Princess Leia is going _____ visit Han.

up

Say the sight word **up**.
Trace and then write the word **up**.

Where is C-3PO?
Write **up** to tell where C-3PO is.

C-3PO is climbing the ladder.

down

Say the sight word **down**.
Trace and then write the word **down**.

down

Where is R2-D2?
Write **down** to tell where R2-D2 is.

R2-D2 did not climb up.

He is _____

below.

please

Say the sight word **please**.
Trace and then write the word **please**.

please

Obi-Wan is polite.
Write **please** to complete the sentences.

Will you _____

come with me?

Don't go to

the dark side,

_____ .

play

Say the sight word **play**.
Trace and then write the word **play**.

play

The droid wants to **play** a game with you!
Write **play** to complete the sentences.

Let's _____ ball!

Will you _____
with me?

said

Say the sight word **said**.
Trace and then write the word **said**.

said

Yoda **said** many things to Luke.
Write **said** to complete the sentence.

"May the Force be with you," _____ Yoda.

Cut along the dotted lines to make your own **sight word** flash cards.

I

you

me

my

we

am

a

the

is

are

he

I ran home.

Play with **me**.

I like **you**.

We are friends.

I can write **my** name.

Yoda is **a** Jedi.

I **am** happy.

Luke **is** brave.

I liked **the** movie.

He is fun.

The Wookiees **are** tall.

she	it
and	for
has	on
under	can
do	in
out	here

It is red.

She is clever.

The lightsaber is **for** Anakin.

Han **and** Chewbacca
fly starships.

The book is **on** the table.

Leia **has** a droid.

He **can** dance.

The ball is **under** the table.

I get **in** the car.

I **do** like to draw.

The starship is **here**.

I get **out** of the car.

there	look
one	go
to	up
down	please
play	said

They **look** at the star.

The planet is **there**.

We **go** to the park.

I have **one** nose.

Padmé climbs **up** the tree.

They go **to** the shop.

Fly faster, **please**.

Mace Windu climbs **down** the ladder.

Yoda **said**, "Do. Or do not. There is no try."

We **play** games.

Answers

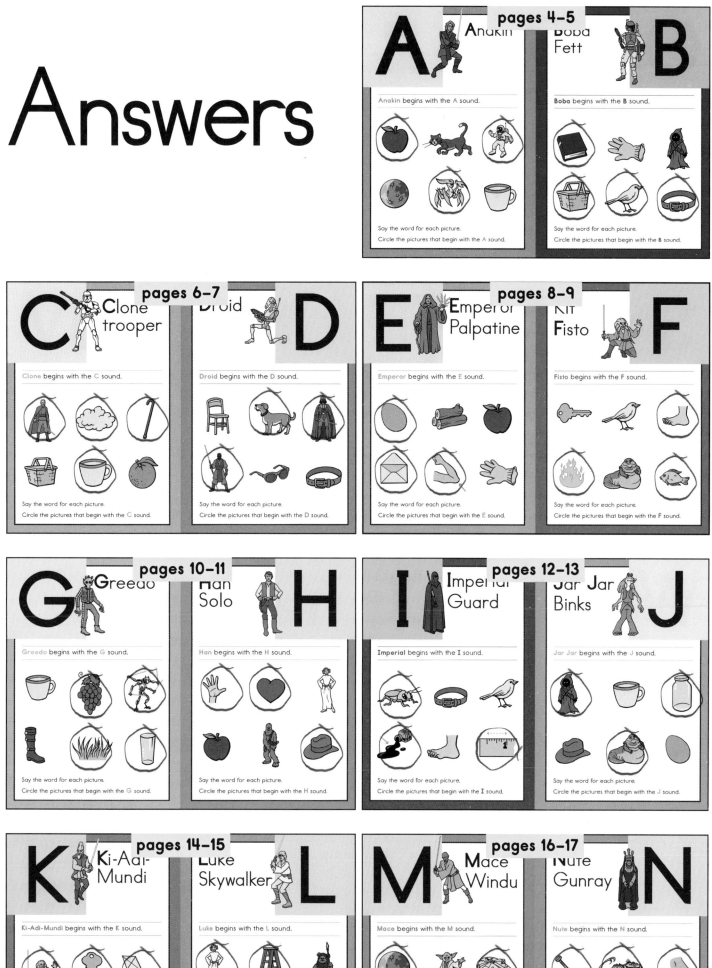

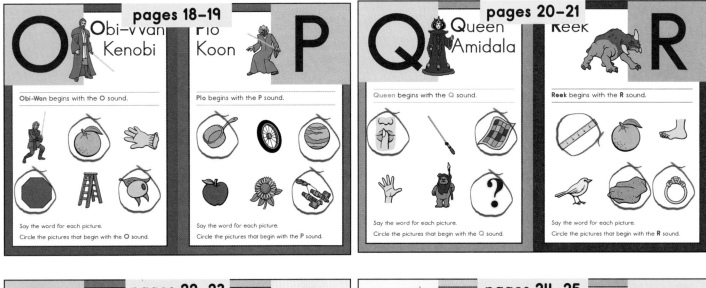

O — Obi-Wan Kenobi

Obi-Wan begins with the O sound.

Say the word for each picture.
Circle the pictures that begin with the O sound.

Plo Koon — P

Plo begins with the P sound.

Say the word for each picture.
Circle the pictures that begin with the P sound.

Q — Queen Amidala

Queen begins with the Q sound.

Say the word for each picture.
Circle the pictures that begin with the Q sound.

Reek — R

Reek begins with the R sound.

Say the word for each picture.
Circle the pictures that begin with the R sound.

S — Stormtrooper

Stormtrooper begins with the S sound.

Say the word for each picture.
Circle the pictures that begin with the S sound.

Tusken Raider — T

Tusken begins with the T sound.

Say the word for each picture.
Circle the pictures that begin with the T sound.

U — Luminara Unduli

Unduli begins with the U sound.

Say the word for each picture.
Circle the pictures that begin with the U sound.

Vader — V

Vader begins with the V sound.

Say the word for each picture.
Circle the pictures that begin with the V sound.

W — Wookiee

Wookiee begins with the W sound.

Say the word for each picture.
Circle the pictures that begin with the W sound.

X-wing — X

X-wing begins with the X sound.

Say the word for each picture.
Circle the pictures that begin with the X sound.

Y — Yoda

Yoda begins with the Y sound.

Say the word for each picture.
Circle the pictures that begin with the Y sound.

Zam Wesell — Z

Zam begins with the Z sound.

Say the word for each picture.
Circle the pictures that begin with the Z sound.

Short a

The first a in Acklay has the short a sound.

Circle the pictures that have the same short a sound as acklay.

Short e

Jedi has the short e sound.

Circle the pictures that have the same short e sound as Jedi.

Short i

Wicket has the short i sound.

Circle the pictures that have the same short i sound as Wicket.

Short o

Podracer has the short o sound.

Circle the pictures that have the same short o sound as podracer.

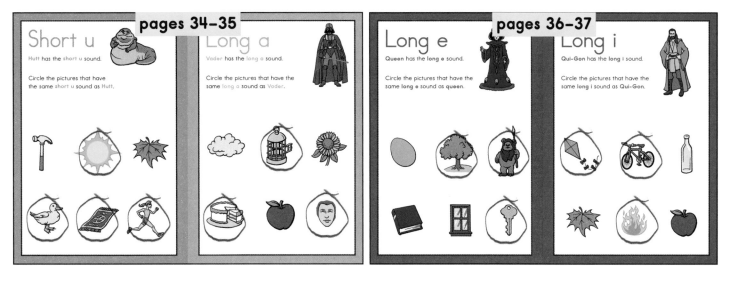

Short u

Hutt has the **short u** sound.

Circle the pictures that have the same short u sound as Hutt.

Long a

Vader has the **long a** sound.

Circle the pictures that have the same long a sound as Vader.

Long e

Queen has the **long e** sound.

Circle the pictures that have the same long e sound as queen.

Long i

Qui-Gon has the **long i** sound.

Circle the pictures that have the same long i sound as Qui-Gon.

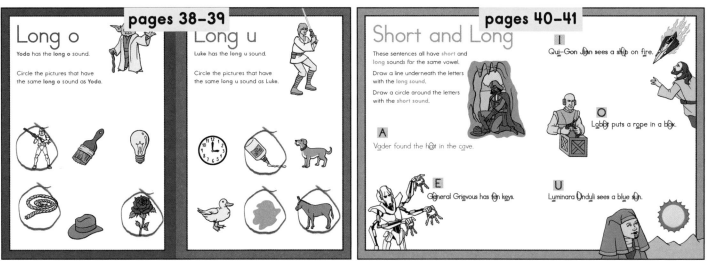

Long o

Yoda has the **long o** sound.

Circle the pictures that have the same long o sound as Yoda.

Long u

Luke has the **long u** sound.

Circle the pictures that have the same long u sound as Luke.

Short and Long

These sentences all have short and long sounds for the same vowel.

Draw a line underneath the letters with the long sound.

Draw a circle around the letters with the short sound.

I
Qui-Gon Jinn sees a ship on fire.

O
Lobot puts a rope in a box.

A
Vader found the hat in the cave.

E
General Grievous has ten keys.

U
Luminara Unduli sees a blue sun.

y

The letter y can have two sounds: a long i sound, or a long e sound.

Draw a box around the pictures that end with the long i sound.

Draw a circle around the pictures that end with the long e sound.

sky lady cry

fly city baby

ch

When c and h are next to each other, they come together to make a new sound: ch.

Say the word for each picture.

Circle the pictures that begin with the ch sound.

Chewbacca

Chewbacca begins with the **ch** sound.

sh

When s and h are next to each other, they come together to make a new sound: sh.

Say the word for each picture.

Circle the pictures that begin with the sh sound.

Shmi

Shmi begins with the **sh** sound.

th

When t and h are next to each other, they come together to make a new sound: th.

Say the word for each picture.

Circle the pictures that begin or end with the th sound.

Darth

Darth ends with the **th** sound.

Names

Say the name of each character.
What is the first sound you hear?
Write the letter that makes that sound.

Luke Skywalker

Yoda

Han Solo

Jabba the Hutt

Princess Leia

Anakin

Jar Jar Binks

Padmé

Darth Maul

Mace Windu

Colour Rhyme!

Each of the colours rhymes with one of the pictures.

Draw a line from each colour to its rhyming picture.

Rhyme Time!

Each of the pictures in the left column rhymes with one of the pictures in the right column.

Draw a line from each picture on the left to its rhyming picture on the right.

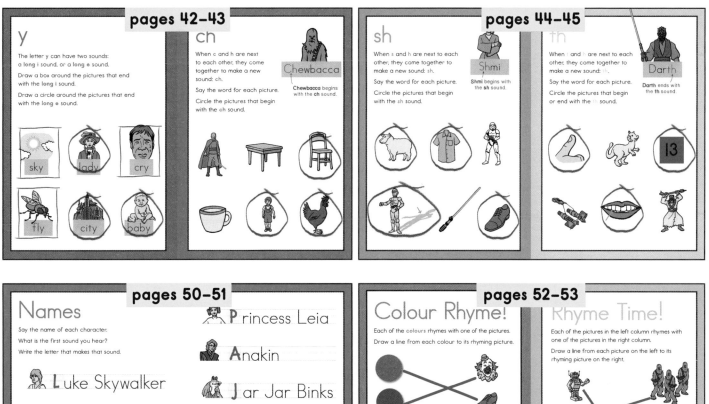

b, d and f

These people, creatures, and things all start with the b, d or f sound.

Say the word for each picture. What beginning sound do you hear?

Write the letter.

d ewback

f oot

b antha

b ox

d roid

Boba **F** ett

d ancer

f ire

d esert

b oy

h, j and k

These people, creatures and things all start with the h, j or k sound.

Say the word for each picture. What beginning sound do you hear?

Write the letter.

h elmet

j ar

k ing

H an

h and

h ug

j ump

k ite

k ick

j unk

m and n

These people, creatures and things all start with the m or n sound.

Say the word for each picture. What beginning sound do you hear?

Write the letter.

m oon

n est

M ace

N ute

m an

n ine

n ose

m ug

m ynock

n exu

r, s and t

These creatures and things all start with the r, s or t sound.

Say the word for each picture. What beginning sound do you hear?

Write the letter.

r eek

s tarship

s tormtrooper

T usken Raider

s poon

t auntaun

t oes

s even

t riangle

r ancor

v, w, x, y and z

These people, creatures and things all start with the v, w, x, y or z sound.

Say the word for each picture. What beginning sound do you hear?

Write the letter.

V ader

W ookiee

w ampa

w ool

X -wing

Y oda

Z am Wesell

z ip

v olcano

x -ray

b or d?

The words for these pictures all end in b or d.

Say the word for each picture. What ending sound do you hear?

Write the letter.

droi **d**

bathtu **b**

san **d**

Bi **b** Fortuna

m or n?

The words for these pictures all end in m or n.

Say the word for each picture. What ending sound do you hear?

Write the letter.

moo **n**

Anaki **n**

dru **m**

Zam Wesell

p or t?

The words for these pictures all end in p or t.

Say the word for each picture. What ending sound do you hear?

Write the letter.

starshi **p**

Lobo **t**

ma **p**

plane **t**

r or s?

The words for these pictures all end in r or s.

Say the word for each picture. What ending sound do you hear?

Write the letter.

ca **r**

sta **r**

Jar Jar Bink **s**

bu **s**

g or k?

The words for these pictures all end in g or k.

Say the word for each picture. What ending sound do you hear?

Write the letter.

ree **k**

fla **g**

do **g**

boo **k**